From Cotton to T-Shirt

by Avery Toolen

Bullfrog Books

Ideas for Parents and Teachers

Bullfrog Books let children practice reading informational text at the earliest reading levels. Repetition, familiar words, and photo labels support early readers.

Before Reading

• Discuss the cover photo. What does it tell them?

• Look at the picture glossary together. Read and discuss the words.

Read the Book

• "Walk" through the book and look at the photos. Let the child ask questions. Point out the photo labels.

• Read the book to the child, or have him or her read independently.

After Reading

• Prompt the child to think more. Ask: Do you have a favorite T-shirt? Have you ever thought about where it came from?

Bullfrog Books are published by Jump!
5357 Penn Avenue South
Minneapolis, MN 55419
www.jumplibrary.com

Library of Congress Cataloging-in-Publication Data

Names: Toolen, Avery, author.
Title: From cotton to T-shirt / by Avery Toolen.
Description: Minneapolis, MN: Jump!, Inc., 2022.
Series: Where does it come from?
Audience: Ages 5–8 | Audience: Grades K–1
Identifiers: LCCN 2020049693 (print)
LCCN 2020049694 (ebook)
ISBN 9781645279730 (hardcover)
ISBN 9781645279747 (paperback)
ISBN 9781645279754 (ebook)
Subjects: LCSH: T-shirt industry—Juvenile literature.
Classification: LCC HD9969.S6 T66 2022 (print)
LCC HD9969.S6 (ebook) | DDC 687/.115—dc23
LC record available at https://lccn.loc.gov/2020049693
LC ebook record available at https://lccn.loc.gov/2020049694

Editor: Eliza Leahy
Designer: Michelle Sonnek

Photo Credits: ithinksky/iStock, cover (left); Iringa Rogova/Shutterstock, cover (right); Ines Behrens-Kunkel/Shutterstock, 1; Muenchbach/Shutterstock, 3; Ranta Images/Shutterstock, 4; Trong Nguyen/Shutterstock, 5, 23tl; lourencolf/Shutterstock, 6–7, 22tl; 23tr; Scott Olson/Getty, 8–9, 22tr, 23bl; DZMITRY PALUBIATKA/Shutterstock, 10; junrong/Shutterstock, 11; Aleksandr Kurganov/Shutterstock, 12–13, 22mr, 23bm; paparazzza/Shutterstock, 14; ANAID studio/Shutterstock, 15, 22br, 23tm; AdaCo/Shutterstock, 16–17, 22bl, 23br; Sabaidee/Shutterstock, 18–19; SDI Productions/iStock, 20–21, 22ml; Surrphoto/Shutterstock, 24.

Printed in the United States of America at Corporate Graphics in North Mankato, Minnesota.

Table of Contents

Ella wears a T-shirt. Where does it come from?

4

cotton
plant

Cotton!
It grows in fields.

cotton
field

Machines pick it.

It goes in a gin.

The gin takes out seeds.

Cool!

cotton
gin

9

Cotton goes to a factory.

factory

A machine spins it.
This makes yarn.
Yarn goes on spools.

yarn

spool

fabric

knitting machine

A machine knits it.

It makes fabric.

It is washed.

This makes it soft.

washing machine

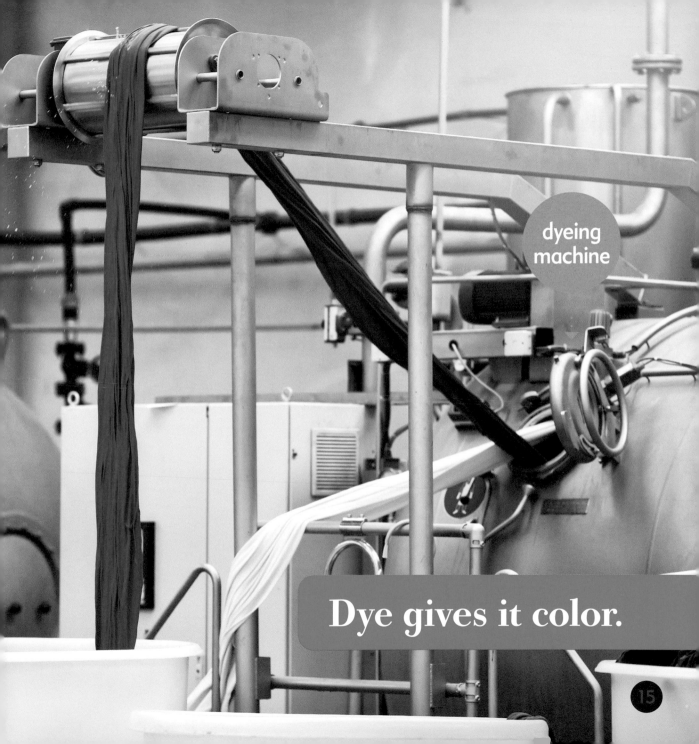

dyeing machine

Dye gives it color.

Then it is cut.
Workers sew it.
They make T-shirts!

sewing
machine

T-shirts are packed.

They go to stores.

We shop.
We buy one!

From Field to Store

How does cotton go from the field to the store? Take a look!

1. Cotton grows in fields. Machines pick it.

2. A cotton gin takes out seeds.

3. Cotton is spun into yarn and knitted into fabric.

4. Fabric is washed and dyed.

5. Fabric is cut and sewn into T-shirts.

6. T-shirts are shipped to stores. We buy them!

Picture Glossary

cotton
A plant that produces fluffy white fibers.

dye
A substance used to change the color of something.

fields
Open pieces of land used for growing crops or for grazing animals.

gin
A machine that separates seeds and other material from cotton.

knits
Makes fabric out of yarn.

sew
To make, repair, or fasten something with stitches made by a needle and thread.

Index

To Learn More

Finding more information is as easy as 1, 2, 3.

❶ Go to www.factsurfer.com

❷ Enter "fromcottontoT-shirt" into the search box.

❸ Choose your book to see a list of websites.